The Sweet & Sav

Waffle Cookbook

All-Day Every-Way Waffle Recipes

BY: SOPHIA FREEMAN

Table of Contents

Introduction

Historians trace the beginnings of waffles to ancient Greece's Obelios cakes. The kind of flat cake was made by roasting batter between two metal plates over an open fire. Eventually, people began using plates with customized designs.

Forged cooking irons originally had a hinged design. The honeycomb pattern first appeared in waffle irons in the 13th century. It was also around the time that the term waffles was first used in print. The term originated from "gaufre," a French word that translated to the Old English word "wafla."

By the 16th century, waffles had become popular in the streets of Europe and across all socio-economic households. The poor made do with just water and flour, and the richer ones used milk, honey, and eggs.

Over the years, waffles have become a kitchen staple. At present, there are three main types of waffles. Belgian or Brussels waffles are leavened with yeast. The crispy and light waffles feature deep ridges.

Predating Belgian waffles, the Liege is a denser and softer variant. It is also sweeter owing to the use of caramelized sugar for coating.

Instead of yeast, American waffles are leavened with baking powder.

Additional Useful & Interesting Information

There are not one but three dates to commemorate waffles: International Waffle Day on March 25, National Waffle Day on August 24 (Cornelius Swarthout received the first US patent on the waffle iron on August 24, 1869), and National Waffle Week on the second week of September.

The first electric waffle iron featured a thermostat that addressed overheating and burning. Thomas J. Stackbeck designed the device for General Electric (GE) in 1911. The modern waffle irons continue to utilize the mechanism coupled with other safety and user-friendly features such as lighter-weight materials, non-stick surfaces, and removable plates.

Eggo frozen toaster waffles were called "Froffles" when the Dorsa Brothers first brought them into the US supermarkets in 1953. Customers began calling them "Eggos" for their eggy flavor. The name was later officially adopted in 1955.

Fluffy Waffles with Cinnamon Syrup

Waking up to fluffy waffles is a great way to start the day. The secret to making waffles fluffy is beating the egg whites until you see stiff peaks forming. In this recipe, you'll also learn how to make creamy cinnamon syrup, which makes the waffles even more delicious.

Serving Size: 10

Preparation & Cooking Time: 10 minutes

Ingredients:

- 2 cups all-purpose flour
- 1 tablespoon sugar
- ½ teaspoon salt
- 2 teaspoons baking powder
- 3 egg yolks
- ¼ cup vegetable oil
- 2 cups milk
- 3 egg whites

Cinnamon syrup

- ½ cup corn syrup
- ¼ cup water
- 1 cup sugar
- 5 oz. evaporated milk
- ½ teaspoon ground cinnamon
- 1 teaspoon vanilla extract

For serving

- Blackberries
- Sliced strawberries

Instructions:

First, in a bowl, mix the flour, baking powder, sugar and salt.

In another bowl, beat the egg yolks, oil and milk.

Pour the egg yolk mixture into the flour mixture.

Mix well.

Beat the egg whites using an electric mixer until you see stiff peaks forming.

Add this to the batter.

Preheat your waffle iron.

Next, pour the batter into the waffle maker and bake according to manufacturer's instructions.

To make the syrup, add the corn syrup and water to a pan over medium heat.

Stir in the sugar.

Bring to a boil.

Next, reduce heat and simmer while stirring until the syrup has thickened.

Turn off the heat.

Pour in the milk.

Then, stir in the ground cinnamon and vanilla extract.

Serve the waffles with the cinnamon syrup and fresh berries.

Nutrients per Serving:

- Calories 424
- Fat 12 g
- Saturated fat 4 g
- Carbohydrates 71 g
- Fiber 1 g
- Protein 9 g
- Cholesterol 94 mg
- Sugars 41 g
- Sodium 344 mg
- Potassium 554 mg

Buttermilk Waffles

Serve these for breakfast at home, and for sure, you'll never hear the end of how great the buttermilk waffles are. To complete the dish, drizzle with strawberry syrup and top with whipped cream and fresh strawberry slices.

Serving Size: 16

Preparation & Cooking Time: 30 minutes

Ingredients:

- 1 ¾ cups all-purpose flour
- ½ teaspoon salt
- 1 teaspoon baking soda
- 1 teaspoon baking powder
- 2 eggs
- 1/3 cup canola oil
- 2 cups buttermilk

For serving

- Whipped cream
- Strawberry syrup

Instructions:

First, in a bowl, mix the flour, baking soda, baking powder and salt.

Beat the eggs in another bowl.

Stir in the oil and buttermilk.

Next, add the flour mixture to the egg mixture, stirring.

Cook in the waffle iron according to manufacturer's instructions.

Then, top the waffles with whipped cream and fresh strawberry slices.

Drizzle with the strawberry syrup before serving.

Nutrients per Serving:

- Calories 223
- Fat 11 g
- Saturated fat 2 g
- Carbohydrates 24 g
- Fiber 1 g
- Protein 6 g
- Cholesterol 56 mg
- Sugars 4 g
- Sodium 435 mg
- Potassium 200 mg

Bacon & Cheese Waffles

Adding bacon and cheese to the waffle batter takes your waffles to a whole new level. As they say, almost everything is better with bacon. And who doesn't want extra cheese?

Serving Size: 12

Preparation & Cooking Time: 20 minutes

Ingredients:

- 2 cups pancake mix
- 1 egg
- 1 tablespoon butter, melted
- 1 cup sour cream
- 1 cup milk
- 1 cup cheddar cheese, shredded
- 8 bacon strips, cooked crisp and crumbled

Instructions:

Add the pancake mix to a bowl.

In another bowl, beat the egg, butter, sour cream and milk.

Pour the egg mixture into the pancake mix.

Fold in the cheese and bacon.

Bake in the waffle maker according to manufacturer's instructions.

Nutrients per Serving:

- Calories 370
- Fat 20 g
- Saturated fat 12 g
- Carbohydrates 32 g
- Fiber 2 g
- Protein 13 g
- Cholesterol 98 mg
- Sugars 10 g
- Sodium 773 mg
- Potassium 250 mg

Pumpkin Waffles

These golden pumpkin waffles are truly delightful. They're sweet with a hint of citrus flavor. And they're fluffy, too, just the way you like them. Top your waffles with orange walnut butter and serve with your favorite hotdogs or sausages.

Serving Size: 4

Preparation & Cooking Time: 20 minutes

Ingredients:

Orange butter

- 1 tablespoon orange zest
- ½ cup butter, softened
- ¼ cup walnuts, chopped

Waffles

- 1 cup all-purpose flour
- ¼ teaspoon baking soda
- ½ teaspoon baking powder
- 2 tablespoons brown sugar
- 1 teaspoon ground cinnamon
- ½ teaspoon salt
- 2 eggs
- 1 cup milk
- 2 tablespoons butter
- ½ cup canned pumpkin puree

For serving

- Maple syrup or honey

Instructions:

Preheat your waffle iron.

In a bowl, combine the orange zest, butter and walnuts. Set aside.

To prepare the waffles, mix the flour, baking soda, baking powder, brown sugar, ground cinnamon and salt.

In another bowl, beat the eggs and milk.

Stir in the butter and pumpkin puree.

Add the egg mixture to the flour mixture.

Stir to combine.

Bake the waffles in the waffle maker according to manufacturer's instructions.

Top with the orange butter.

Drizzle with the honey or maple syrup.

Nutrients per Serving:

- Calories 536
- Fat 38 g
- Saturated fat 20 g
- Carbohydrates 41 g
- Fiber 3 g
- Protein 11 g
- Cholesterol 174 mg
- Sugars 11 g
- Sodium 731 mg
- Potassium 286 mg

Oatmeal Waffles

Healthy and tasty waffles loaded with fiber—these are great not only for breakfast but at any time during the day. Top with fresh berries to add more nutrients to your meal.

Serving Size: 6

Preparation & Cooking Time: 30 minutes

Ingredients:

- 1 cup oats
- 1 ½ cups all-purpose flour
- ½ teaspoon ground cinnamon
- 3 teaspoons baking powder
- ¼ teaspoon salt
- 1 ½ cups milk
- 2 eggs, beaten
- 2 tablespoons brown sugar
- 6 tablespoons butter, melted

For serving

- Plain Greek yogurt
- Raspberries
- Blackberries

Instructions:

Mix the oats, flour, ground cinnamon, baking powder and salt in a bowl.

In another bowl, whisk together the milk, eggs, brown sugar and butter.

Pour the milk mixture into the first bowl.

Stir until moistened.

Pour the batter into your waffle maker.

Seal and cook according to the manufacturer's instructions.

Top with the yogurt and berries before serving.

Nutrients per Serving:

- Calories 344
- Fat 16 g
- Saturated fat 9 g
- Carbohydrates 41 g
- Fiber 2 g
- Protein 9 g
- Cholesterol 99 mg
- Sugars 8 g
- Sodium 482 mg
- Potassium 398 mg

Waffle Dippers with Peaches & Cream

Ideal whether for breakfast, brunch or snack, these waffle dippers are more special, thanks to the creamy peach dip that you'll surely love. You can also sprinkle with ground cinnamon and toasted walnuts or pecans to add extra flavor and crunch to your waffle strips.

Serving Size: 6

Preparation & Cooking Time: 30 minutes

Ingredients:

- 1 cup all-purpose flour
- 1 cup milk
- 1 teaspoon baking powder
- 1 tablespoon sugar
- ¼ teaspoon salt
- 2 egg yolks
- 2 tablespoons butter, melted
- ¼ teaspoon vanilla extract
- 1 ¼ cups peaches, chopped and divided
- 2 egg whites
- ¾ cup peach yogurt
- 2 cups whipped cream (sweetened)

For serving

- Ground cinnamon
- Toasted walnuts or pecans

Instructions:

First, in a bowl, combine the flour, baking powder, sugar and salt.

In another bowl, beat the egg yolks and stir in the butter, milk and vanilla extract.

Add the egg mixture to the flour mixture.

Stir to blend.

Fold in 1 cup peaches.

Next, beat the egg whites with an electric mixer until you see stiff peaks forming.

Add this to the batter.

Bake the batter in your waffle maker according to the manufacturer's instructions.

Let cool.

Then, slice the waffles into strips.

Prepare the dip by mixing the yogurt, whipped cream and remaining peaches.

Serve the waffle strips with the dip, and top with ground cinnamon and toasted nuts.

Nutrients per Serving:

- Calories 341
- Fat 21 g
- Saturated fat 13 g
- Carbohydrates 30 g
- Fiber 1 g
- Protein 8 g
- Cholesterol 122 mg
- Sugars 14 g
- Sodium 279 mg
- Potassium 325 mg

Gingerbread Waffles

Jazz up your mornings with these sweet spicy gingerbread waffles with rich cream cheese frosting.

Serving Size: 6

Preparation & Cooking Time: 30 minutes

Ingredients:

- 2 oz. cream cheese, softened
- ½ cup butter, softened
- ½ teaspoon vanilla extract
- 2 tablespoons milk
- 1 ½ cups confectioners' sugar
- Pinch salt

Waffles

- 2 cups all-purpose flour
- 1 teaspoon baking soda
- 3 teaspoons baking powder
- ¼ cup brown sugar
- 1 teaspoon ground cinnamon
- 1 ½ teaspoons ground ginger
- ¼ teaspoon ground nutmeg
- ½ teaspoon salt
- 4 egg yolks
- ½ cup butter, melted
- 2 teaspoons vanilla extract
- ½ cup molasses
- 2 cups buttermilk
- 4 egg whites

Instructions:

First, beat the cream cheese and butter in a bowl.

Stir in the vanilla, milk, sugar and salt.

Cover the bowl. Set aside.

Next, combine the flour, baking soda, baking powder, sugar, cinnamon, ginger, nutmeg and salt in another bowl.

In a third bowl, beat the butter, egg yolks, vanilla, molasses and buttermilk.

Add this to the flour mixture and stir.

Next, use an electric mixer to beat the egg whites until soft peaks form.

Add this to the batter.

Pour the batter into your waffle maker.

Then, cook the waffles according to the manufacturer's instructions.

Spread the cream cheese mixture on top and serve.

Nutrients per Serving:

- Calories 776
- Fat 38 g
- Saturated fat 23 g
- Carbohydrates 97 g
- Fiber 1 g
- Protein 12 g
- Cholesterol 219 mg
- Sugars 63 g
- Sodium 1188 mg
- Potassium 911 mg

Hawaiian Waffles

Bring tropical flavors to your breakfast meal with these Hawaiian waffles topped with shredded coconut and pineapple chunks.

Serving Size: 16

Preparation & Cooking Time: 30 minutes

Ingredients:

Topping

- ½ cup corn syrup
- ¼ cup pineapple juice
- 20 oz. pineapple chunks, undrained
- ½ cup coconut flakes (sweetened)
- ½ cup sugar

Waffles

- 2 cups all-purpose flour
- 1 tablespoon sugar
- 4 teaspoons baking powder
- ½ teaspoon salt
- 2 egg yolks
- ¼ cup butter, melted
- 1 cup milk
- ¼ cup macadamia nuts, chopped
- ¼ cup coconut flakes (sweetened)
- 8 oz. pineapple chunks, drained
- 2 egg whites

Instructions:

Prepare the topping by adding the corn syrup, pineapple juice, pineapple chunks, coconut flakes and sugar in a pan over medium heat.

Bring to a boil.

Reduce heat and simmer for 15 minutes.

Next, in a bowl, mix the flour, sugar, baking powder and salt.

In another bowl, beat the egg yolks, butter and milk.

Add the egg yolk mixture to the flour mixture. Then, mix.

Next, fold in the macadamia nuts, coconut flakes and pineapple chunks.

Then, beat the egg whites with an electric mixer until you see stiff peaks forming.

Add this to the batter.

Pour the batter into your waffle maker.

Bake according to the manufacturer's instructions.

Lastly, top the waffles with the syrup and serve.

Nutrients per Serving:

- Calories 446
- Fat 14 g
- Saturated fat 8 g
- Carbohydrates 76 g
- Fiber 2 g
- Protein 7 g
- Cholesterol 73 mg
- Sugars 43 g
- Sodium 495 mg
- Potassium 442 mg

Pecan Waffles

You won't want to miss breakfast if you're expecting these fluffy and delicious waffles made with wheat bran and pecans.

Serving Size: 6

Preparation & Cooking Time: 30 minutes

Ingredients:

- ¼ cup wheat bran
- 1 ¼ cups all-purpose flour
- 2 ½ teaspoons baking powder
- 1 tablespoon sugar
- ½ teaspoon salt
- 1 egg white
- 1 egg
- 2 tablespoons canola oil
- 1 ½ cups milk
- 1/3 cup pecans, chopped

Instructions:

Add the wheat bran, flour, baking powder, sugar and salt to a bowl and mix.

In another bowl, beat the egg white, egg, canola oil and milk.

Add this to the wheat bran mixture.

Fold in the pecans.

Cook the waffles in your waffle maker according to the manufacturer's instructions.

Nutrients per Serving:

- Calories 227
- Fat 10 g
- Saturated fat 1 g
- Carbohydrates 28 g
- Fiber 2 g
- Protein 7 g
- Cholesterol 32 mg
- Sugars 6 g
- Sodium 444 mg
- Potassium 320 mg

Ginger & Cinnamon Waffles

Here's another simple and straightforward waffle recipe that you can serve at breakfast or any time during the day.

Serving Size: 8

Preparation & Cooking Time: 30 minutes

Ingredients:

- 1 cup all-purpose flour
- 1/8 teaspoon ground cloves
- ¾ teaspoon ground cinnamon
- ½ teaspoon baking soda
- 1 teaspoon ground ginger
- 1 ½ teaspoons baking powder
- ¼ teaspoon salt
- 1 egg yolk
- 1/3 cup brown sugar
- ¾ cup buttermilk
- 3 tablespoons butter, melted
- ¼ cup molasses
- 1 egg white
- 1/8 teaspoon cream of tartar
- Confectioners' sugar

Instructions:

First, mix the flour, baking powder, baking powder, cinnamon, ginger, cloves and salt.

In another bowl, beat the egg yolk, brown sugar, buttermilk, butter and molasses.

Add this to the flour mixture.

Next, beat the egg white and cream of tartar using an electric mixer until you see stiff peaks forming.

Pour this into the batter.

Add the batter to your waffle maker.

Then, cook the waffles according to the manufacturer's instructions.

Dust with the confectioners' sugar before serving.

Nutrients per Serving:

- Calories 353
- Fat 11 g
- Saturated fat 6 g
- Carbohydrates 59 g
- Fiber 1 g
- Protein 6 g
- Cholesterol 78 mg
- Sugars 33 g
- Sodium 621 mg
- Potassium 627 mg

Apple Spice Waffles

Waking up to the aroma of these apple spice waffles is something you'd look forward to each morning. Be sure to top with whipped cream, maple syrup and chopped apple.

Serving Size: 12

Preparation & Cooking Time: 30 minutes

Ingredients:

- 2 cups biscuit mix
- 1 teaspoon ground nutmeg
- 2 teaspoons ground cinnamon
- 2 eggs
- 6 tablespoons butter, melted
- 1 ½ cups milk
- 1 cup apple, chopped

For serving

- Whipped cream
- Chopped apples
- Maple syrup

Instructions:

Preheat your waffle iron.

In a bowl, combine the biscuit mix, ground nutmeg and ground cinnamon.

Beat the eggs in another bowl.

Stir in the butter and milk.

Add the egg mixture to the biscuit mixture.

Stir until moistened.

Fold in the apples.

Bake the waffles according to the manufacturer's instructions.

Top with the whipped cream and chopped apples.

Drizzle with the maple syrup and serve.

Nutrients per Serving:

- Calories 321
- Fat 19 g
- Saturated fat 10 g
- Carbohydrates 34 g
- Fiber 2 g
- Protein 7 g
- Cholesterol 97 mg
- Sugars 6 g
- Sodium 558 mg
- Potassium 180 mg

BLT Waffles with Egg

Bacon, lettuce and tomato sandwich is popular all over the world. Make the waffle version of the sandwich, top it with a sunny side up egg and garnish with chopped parsley for a wonderful breakfast dish for you and your family.

Serving Size: 4

Preparation & Cooking Time: 30 minutes

Ingredients:

Waffles

- 1 cup all-purpose flour
- 1 teaspoon baking powder
- ½ teaspoon salt
- 1 egg yolk
- 1 cup milk
- 1/8 cup vegetable oil
- 1 egg white

Topping

- 8 bacon slices
- 4 eggs
- 4 cups Romaine lettuce, chopped
- 1 tomato, sliced
- ½ cup cheddar cheese, shredded

Garnish

- Chopped parsley

Instructions:

First, prepare the waffles by mixing first the dry ingredients in a bowl.

Second, combine the flour, baking powder and salt.

In another bowl, beat the egg yolk, milk and oil.

Add this to the flour mixture.

Use an electric mixer to beat the egg white until you see stiff peaks forming.

Add this to the batter.

Next, pour the batter into the waffle maker.

Bake according to manufacturer's instructions.

While waiting, add the bacon to a pan over medium heat.

Cook until crispy.

Drain on a plate lined with paper towel.

Then, cook the egg sunny side up in the same pan with the bacon drippings.

Cook until the egg whites are set.

Place the waffles on a serving plate.

Top with the lettuce, tomato slices, bacon, egg and cheese.

Sprinkle with the chopped parsley on top.

Nutrients per Serving:

- Calories 382
- Fat 26 g
- Saturated fat 9 g
- Carbohydrates 3 g
- Fiber 2 g
- Protein 18 g
- Cholesterol 228 mg
- Sugars 3 g
- Sodium 695 mg
- Potassium 400 mg

Waffles with Ham, Egg & Asparagus

These savory waffles topped with cubed ham steak, chopped asparagus and sunny side up egg, sprinkled with grated Gruyere cheese would certainly up the ante of your breakfast.

Serving Size: 6

Preparation & Cooking Time: 1 hour

Ingredients:

- 16 asparagus, trimmed and sliced
- ¼ cup green onions, chopped
- Salt and pepper to taste
- 9 eggs
- 2 cups all-purpose flour
- 1 tablespoon baking powder
- 6 tablespoons butter, melted
- 1 ½ cups milk
- 1 cup Gruyere cheese, grated and divided
- 12 oz. cooked ham steak, sliced into cubes

Instructions:

Preheat your oven to 350 degrees F.

Spread the asparagus and onions in a baking pan.

Season with the salt and pepper.

Roast in the oven for 10 minutes.

Let cool and set aside.

Take 3 eggs and separate egg whites form the yolks.

In a bowl, combine the flour, baking powder and salt.

In another bowl, beat the egg yolks. Then, stir in the butter and milk.

Add this to the flour mixture.

Use an electric mixer to beat the egg whites until you see stiff peaks forming.

Add this to the batter.

Fold in half of the asparagus mixture and ¾ cup cheese.

Pour the batter into the waffle maker.

Bake according to the manufacturer's instructions.

Fry the remaining eggs sunny side up in a pan over medium heat.

Serve the waffles topped with the eggs, ham cubes, remaining asparagus mixture, and remaining Gruyere cheese.

Nutrients per Serving:

- Calories 544
- Fat 29 g
- Saturated fat 15 g
- Carbohydrates 38 g
- Fiber 2 g
- Protein 33 g
- Cholesterol 364 mg
- Sugars 4 g
- Sodium 993 mg
- Potassium 615 mg

Chocolate Chip & Cherry Waffles

Create these sweet and yummy chocolate cherry waffles without any hassle with their recipe that only takes 30 minutes to prepare.

Serving Size: 6

Preparation & Cooking Time: 30 minutes

Ingredients:

Syrup

- ½ cup sweet cherries, pitted and chopped
- ½ cup sugar
- ½ cup water
- 1 tablespoon cornstarch

Waffles

- 1 ¼ cups all-purpose flour
- 1 teaspoon baking soda
- 1 teaspoon baking powder
- 1 teaspoon ground cinnamon
- 2 eggs
- 1 ½ cups buttermilk
- ½ teaspoon almond extract
- 1/3 cup canola oil
- ½ cup chocolate chips
- 1 ½ cups sweet cherries, pitted and chopped

Instructions:

Preheat your waffle iron.

Add the sweet cherries to a pan over medium heat.

Stir in the sugar and water.

Bring to a boil.

Next, reduce heat and simmer for 5 minutes, stirring often.

Stir in the cornstarch.

Cook while stirring for 1 minute.

Turn off heat and set aside.

Next, in a bowl, combine the flour, baking soda, baking powder and ground cinnamon.

In another bowl, whisk together the eggs, butter milk, almond extract and oil.

Then, add the egg mixture to the flour mixture and stir.

Fold in the chocolate chips and cherries.

Pour the batter into the waffle maker.

Bake according to the manufacturer's instructions.

Serve with the cherry syrup.

Nutrients per Serving:

- Calories 428
- Fat 19 g
- Saturated fat 4 g
- Carbohydrates 59 g
- Fiber 2 g
- Protein 8 g
- Cholesterol 64 mg
- Sugars 33 g
- Sodium 432 mg
- Potassium 278 mg

Chocolate Chip Waffles

Expect these chocolate chip waffles to be a big hit each time you serve them at home. It'd definitely be a good idea to make a big batch of them and freeze some for later use. Simply reheat the frozen waffles in a waffle maker before serving.

Serving Size: 12

Preparation & Cooking Time: 20 minutes

Ingredients:

- ¼ cup oats
- ¾ cup whole wheat flour
- 1 ¼ cups all-purpose flour
- 2 teaspoons baking powder
- 1 teaspoon sugar
- ¼ teaspoon salt
- 2 eggs
- 1 tablespoon butter, melted
- 1 1/3 cups milk
- 1 tablespoon honey
- 2 tablespoons olive oil
- ½ cups chocolate chips

Garnish

- Miniature chocolate chips

Instructions:

Combine the oats, all-purpose flour, whole wheat flour, sugar, baking powder and salt in a bowl.

In another bowl, beat the eggs and stir in the butter, milk, honey and olive oil.

Add the egg mixture to the oat mixture.

Stir until moistened.

Fold in the chocolate chips.

Pour the batter into your waffle maker.

Cook according to the manufacturer's instructions.

Top with the miniature chocolate chips before serving.

Nutrients per Serving:

- Calories 339
- Fat 13 g
- Saturated fat 5 g
- Carbohydrates 49 g
- Fiber 4 g
- Protein 10 g
- Cholesterol 77 mg
- Sugars 15 g
- Sodium 361 mg
- Potassium 330 mg

Stacked Pumpkin Waffles

Stack your pumpkin waffles into a tall tower, spreading a cranberry tower between the layers. For sure, they will impress everyone at the table.

Serving Size: 3

Preparation & Cooking Time: 30 minutes

Ingredients:

- 1 ½ cups all-purpose flour
- 1 teaspoon baking powder
- 1 tablespoon brown sugar
- ¼ teaspoon salt
- 1 egg
- 1 ¼ cups milk
- 4 ½ teaspoons butter, melted
- 2/3 cup canned pumpkin puree
- ¼ cup pecans, toasted and chopped

Cranberry butter

- ¼ cup maple syrup
- ½ cup cranberries
- 1 cup butter, softened

For serving

- Maple syrup

Instructions:

First, add the flour, baking powder, brown sugar and salt to a bowl and stir.

Beat the egg in another bowl.

Stir in the milk, butter and pumpkin puree.

Next, add the egg mixture to the flour mixture.

Stir in the pecans.

Pour the batter into your waffle maker.

Bake according to the manufacturer's instructions.

Next, add the maple syrup and cranberries to a pan over medium heat.

Cook while stirring for 10 minutes.

Transfer to a bowl and let cool.

Then, stir in the butter.

Spread the cranberry butter on one side of the waffles and stack to form a tower.

Nutrients per Serving:

- Calories 595
- Fat 30 g
- Saturated fat 13 g
- Carbohydrates 69 g
- Fiber 5 g
- Protein 14 g
- Cholesterol 115 mg
- Sugars 15 g
- Sodium 557 mg
- Potassium 534 mg

Whole Wheat Waffle with Creamy Chicken Spinach

Pair your whole wheat waffle with creamy chicken and spinach sauce for a savory dish that will leave your tummy satisfied.

Serving Size: 12

Preparation & Cooking Time: 30 minutes

Ingredients:

Sauce

- ¾ cup milk
- 10 ¾ oz. cream of chicken soup
- 10 oz. spinach, rinsed and drained
- 1 ½ cups chicken, cooked and shredded

Waffles

- 3 cups whole wheat flour
- 4 teaspoons baking powder
- 3 tablespoons sugar
- 1 teaspoon salt
- 2 eggs
- ½ cup butter, melted
- 3 cups milk
- 1 cup Swiss cheese, shredded

Instructions:

Add the milk, cream of chicken soup, spinach and chicken to a pan over medium heat.

Cook while stirring for 5 minutes.

Turn off the heat and transfer the mixture to a bowl.

Prepare the waffles by mixing first the flour, baking powder, sugar and salt.

In another bowl, beat the eggs, butter and milk.

Add the egg mixture to the flour mixture and mix.

Fold in the Swiss cheese.

Pour the batter to your waffle maker.

Cook according to the manufacturer's instructions.

Slice the waffle in half and serve with the creamy chicken and spinach sauce.

Nutrients per Serving:

- Calories 335
- Saturated fat 8 g
- Fat 15 g
- Carbohydrates 34 g
- Fiber 5 g
- Protein 15 g
- Cholesterol 52 mg
- Sugars 7 g
- Potassium 442 mg
- Sodium 647 mg

Blueberry Oat Waffle with Bacon Strips

Every bite into this crispy waffle gives you loads of flavors and nutrients. Top with maple syrup, butter and blueberries and pair with strips of crispy bacon.

Serving Size: 4

Preparation & Cooking Time: 30 minutes

Ingredients:

- ½ cup oats
- 2/3 cup all-purpose flour
- 1 teaspoon baking powder
- 1 tablespoon brown sugar
- ½ teaspoon salt
- 1 egg
- 2/3 cup milk
- ½ teaspoon lemon juice
- ¼ cup oil
- ¼ cup pecans, toasted and crushed
- ½ cup blueberries, chopped
- 6 to 8 bacon slices

Topping

- Butter
- Maple syrup
- Fresh blueberries, sliced

Instructions:

Combine the oats, flour, baking powder, brown sugar and salt in a bowl.

Next, beat the egg and milk in another bowl.

Stir in the lemon juice and oil.

Add the egg mixture to the oat mixture and stir.

Fold in the blueberries and crushed pecans.

Let sit for 5 minutes.

Next, add the batter to a waffle maker.

Cook according to the manufacturer's instructions.

Then, cook the bacon strips in a pan over medium heat until crispy.

Top the waffles with the butter and maple syrup.

Sprinkle with the blueberry slices and serve with the crispy bacon strips.

Nutrients per Serving:

- Calories 691
- Fat 44 g
- Saturated fat 5 g
- Carbohydrates 64 g
- Fiber 5 g
- Protein 14 g
- Cholesterol 100 mg
- Sugars 15 g
- Sodium 907 mg
- Potassium 445 mg

Turkey, Bacon & Ham Waffle Sandwich

This is one loaded waffle sandwich with ham, turkey, bacon and apricot preserves. You'll only have good things to say about the delicious waffle sandwich.

Serving Size: 4

Preparation & Cooking Time: 20 minutes

Ingredients:

- ½ cup apricot preserves
- 8 frozen waffles
- 4 deli ham slices
- 4 deli turkey slices
- 4 bacon strips, cooked crispy
- 3 oz. Havarti cheese, sliced
- 2 tablespoons butter

Instructions:

Preheat your waffle maker.

Spread the apricot preserves on one side of the waffles.

Add the ham, turkey and bacon slices on top.

Top with the cheese.

Top with the other waffles.

Spread the top with the butter.

Bake in the waffle maker for 5 minutes per side.

Nutrients per Serving:

- Calories 511
- Fat 23 g
- Saturated fat 10 g
- Carbohydrates 57 g
- Fiber 2 g
- Protein 21 g
- Cholesterol 70 mg
- Sugars 22 g
- Sodium 1163 mg
- Potassium 413 mg

Banana & Nut Waffle Cake

Make a tall tower of waffle cake using this recipe that flavors up the batter with nuts and bananas. Don't forget to drizzle with butterscotch syrup before serving.

Serving Size: 6

Preparation & Cooking Time: 30 minutes

Ingredients:

- ½ cup all-purpose flour
- ½ cup whole wheat flour
- 1 ½ teaspoons baking powder
- 2 tablespoons cornstarch
- ¼ teaspoon salt
- 2 eggs
- 1 tablespoon canola oil
- 1 teaspoon vanilla extract
- ½ cup milk

Butterscotch syrup

- 1 tablespoon corn syrup
- ¾ cup sugar
- 2 tablespoons water
- 1 tablespoon butter
- ¼ cup heavy whipping cream
- ½ teaspoon vanilla extract
- 1 teaspoon ground cinnamon
- Pinch salt

Toppings

- 1 cup sweetened whipped cream
- 2 bananas, sliced
- ½ cup walnuts, toasted and chopped

Instructions:

Preheat your waffle maker.

Combine the all-purpose flour, whole wheat flour, baking powder, cornstarch and salt.

Add the eggs to another bowl. Then, beat.

Stir in the oil, vanilla extract and milk.

Add the wet mixture to the first bowl.

Stir well.

Pour the batter into the waffle iron.

Bake according to the manufacturer's instructions.

To make the butterscotch syrup, simmer the corn syrup, sugar and water in a pan over medium heat.

Cook while stirring for 2 minutes.

Increase heat to medium high and bring to a boil.

Reduce heat and simmer until syrup has thickened.

Turn off the heat.

Stir in the butter, heavy whipping cream, vanilla extract, ground cinnamon and salt.

Place a waffle on a serving plate.

Spread the top side with the whipped cream and butterscotch syrup.

Top with the banana slices and walnuts.

Place another waffle on top. Then, repeat the layers until all ingredients are used.

Nutrients per Serving:

- Calories 535
- Fat 31 g
- Saturated fat 1 g
- Carbohydrates 60 g
- Fiber 4 g
- Protein 9 g
- Cholesterol 104 mg
- Sugars 36 g
- Sodium 509 mg
- Potassium 376 mg

Hash Brown Waffles with Guacamole & Salsa

These crunchy hash brown waffles are a welcome addition to your breakfast menu. You'll love them so much you'll find yourself snacking on them in the afternoon.

Serving Size: 4

Preparation & Cooking Time: 30 minutes

Ingredients:

- 5 eggs, divided
- ½ teaspoon ground cumin
- ¼ teaspoon chili powder
- Salt and pepper to taste
- 1 onion, chopped
- 1 ¾ cups hash browns, shredded
- 2 tablespoons salsa
- ¼ cup green chili, chopped
- 2 tablespoons canola oil

Toppings

- Cheddar cheese, shredded
- Salsa
- Guacamole
- Sour cream
- Chopped cilantro

Instructions:

Beat 1 egg in a bowl.

Stir in the cumin, chili powder, salt and pepper.

Add the onion, potatoes, salsa and green chili.

Mix well.

Pour the batter into your waffle maker.

Cook according to manufacturer's instructions.

Cook the remaining eggs in a pan over medium heat.

Serve the waffles with the fried eggs, cheddar cheese, salsa, guacamole and sour cream.

Sprinkle with the chopped cilantro.

Nutrients per Serving:

- Calories 273
- Fat 17 g
- Saturated fat 5 g
- Carbohydrates 17 g
- Fiber 2 g
- Protein 12 g
- Cholesterol 245 mg
- Sugars 2 g
- Sodium 570 mg
- Potassium 539 mg

Chocolate Pecan Waffles

These chocolate waffles are hard to say no to. They are creamy, fluffy, and a little crunchy, just how you like your waffles. Pecans are added to the batter for extra crunch. Dust with powdered sugar or serve with your favorite fruit.

Serving Size: 4

Preparation & Cooking Time: 30 minutes

Ingredients:

- 2 cups pancake mix
- 2 eggs
- ¼ cup canola oil
- ½ cup chocolate syrup
- 1 ½ cups milk
- 2/3 cup pecans, toasted and chopped

Chocolate butter

- ½ cup confectioners' sugar
- ½ cup butter, softened
- 2 tablespoons cocoa

Instructions:

Add the pancake mix to a bowl.

In another bowl, beat the eggs, oil, chocolate syrup and milk.

Add this to the pancake mix.

Fold in the pecans.

Add the mixture to your waffle maker.

Bake according to manufacturer's instructions.

Combine the chocolate butter ingredients in a bowl.

Serve the waffles with the chocolate butter.

Nutrients per Serving:

- Calories 695
- Fat 47.7 g
- Saturated Fat 18.4 g
- Carbohydrate 60.6 g
- Fiber 3 g
- Protein 10 g
- Cholesterol 155 mg
- Sugars 38 g
- Sodium 507 mg
- Potassium 338 mg

Waffles with Mustard Chicken

Yes, you can pair your favorite fluffy waffles with crispy mustard chicken. Here's a recipe that only requires minimal preparation.

Serving Size: 8

Preparation & Cooking Time: 40 minutes

Ingredients:

- 1/2 cup all-purpose flour
- Salt and pepper to taste
- 4 eggs
- ¼ cup mustard
- 8 chicken thighs
- Oil

Waffles

- 3 teaspoons baking powder
- 2 tablespoons sugar
- 1 ¾ cups all-purpose flour
- 2 eggs
- ½ cup butter, melted
- 1 ¾ cups milk
- 2 teaspoons vanilla extract

For serving

- Maple syrup

Instructions:

In a bowl, mix the flour, salt and pepper.

Add the eggs to another bowl and beat.

Stir in the mustard.

Coat the chicken with the flour.

Next, dip in the egg and cover with the flour mixture once more.

Add the oil to a pan over medium heat.

Fry the chicken for 3 to 5 minutes per side or until golden.

Drain and set aside.

Preheat your waffle maker.

Next, in a bowl, combine the flour, baking powder and sugar.

In another bowl, beat the eggs, butter, milk and vanilla extract.

Then, add the egg mixture to the flour mixture and mix well.

Pour the batter into the waffle maker.

Cook according to the manufacturer's instructions.

Serve the waffles with the chicken and maple syrup.

Nutrients per Serving:

- Calories 576
- Fat 27.3 g
- Saturated Fat 11.7 g
- Cholesterol 247 mg
- Sodium 266 mg
- Carbohydrate 29.4 g
- Fiber 1.5
- Sugars 6.1 g
- Protein 50.9 g
- Potassium 673 mg

Apple Pie Waffles

Turn your favorite apple pie into a waffle and serve it with yogurt and berries. This is an effortless breakfast dish that you can make even during busy mornings.

Serving Size: 6

Preparation & Cooking Time: 35 minutes

Ingredients:

- ¼ cup butter
- 2 tablespoons sugar
- 6 apples, chopped
- 1 teaspoon ground cinnamon
- 1 tablespoon honey
- 1 teaspoon vanilla extract

Waffles

- 2 cups all-purpose flour
- 1 teaspoon baking soda
- 1 tablespoon cornstarch
- 2 tablespoons quick-cooking grits
- Salt to taste
- 2 eggs
- 1 cup ricotta cheese
- 2 cups buttermilk
- 2 teaspoons vanilla extract
- ½ cup oil

For serving

- Yogurt
- Blueberries

Instructions:

First, add the butter to a pan over medium high heat.

Once melted, add the sugar, apples, ground cinnamon, honey and vanilla extract.

Cook while stirring for 10 minutes.

Turn off the heat.

Transfer to a bowl.

Preheat your waffle maker.

Next, in a bowl, mix the flour, baking soda, cornstarch, grits and salt.

In another bowl, beat the eggs and stir in the ricotta, milk, vanilla extract and oil.

Add this to the flour mixture.

Pour the batter into your waffle maker.

Then, cook according to the manufacturer's instructions.

Serve the waffles topped with the apple mixture, yogurt and blueberries.

Nutrients per Serving:

- Calories 633
- Fat 31 g
- Saturated fat 8 g
- Carbohydrates 70 g
- Fiber 4 g
- Protein 18 g
- Cholesterol 96 mg
- Sugars 31 g
- Sodium 709 mg
- Potassium 487 mg

Multi-Grain Waffles

Make your mornings healthier with these multi-grain waffles that you can serve with yogurt and any fresh fruit you have in your kitchen.

Serving Size: 8

Preparation & Cooking Time: 45 minutes

Ingredients:

- ⅔ cup all-purpose flour
- ⅔ cup whole wheat flour
- ½ cup rolled oats
- ¼ cup cornmeal
- 1 ½ teaspoons baking powder
- ½ teaspoon baking soda
- ¼ teaspoon salt
- 1 teaspoon ground cinnamon
- 1 tablespoon canola oil
- 2 eggs
- 2 cups buttermilk
- 2 teaspoons vanilla extract
- ¼ cup brown sugar

For serving

- Yogurt
- Fresh fruits

Instructions:

Combine the all-purpose flour, whole wheat flour, rolled oats, cornmeal, baking soda, baking powder, ground cinnamon and salt in a bowl.

In another bowl, whisk together the eggs, oil, brown sugar and vanilla extract.

Add the wet mixture to the dry mixture and mix well.

Add the batter to your waffle maker.

Cook according to manufacturer's instructions.

Serve with the yogurt and fresh fruits.

Nutrients per Serving:

- Calories 195
- Fat 4.7 g
- Saturated fat 1 g
- Carbohydrates 31.3 g
- Fiber 2.5 g
- Protein 7.9 g
- Cholesterol 49 mg
- Sugars 5 g
- Sodium 379.3 mg
- Potassium 220 mg

Pumpkin & Ginger Waffles

These waffles are perfect for autumn, so you can use fresh pumpkin pureed in a food processor. But if you want to make them at any other time during the year, you can always use canned pumpkin puree. As a health bonus, the waffles are loaded with protein and fiber.

Serving Size: 6

Preparation & Cooking Time: 40 minutes

Ingredients:

- ½ cup all-purpose flour
- ¼ cup coconut flour
- 2 teaspoons baking powder
- ½ teaspoon baking soda
- ¼ cup flaxseed meal
- ½ cup vanilla whey protein powder
- 2 teaspoons arrowroot powder
- ½ teaspoon ground ginger
- 2 teaspoons ground cinnamon
- ¼ cup sugar
- 3 egg whites
- 1 cup almond milk
- 1 tablespoon grapeseed oil
- ¾ cup canned pumpkin puree
- 1 teaspoon vanilla extract
- 1 tablespoon maple syrup
- Whipped dessert topping
- Pinch ground cinnamon

Instructions:

Preheat your waffle maker.

In a bowl, combine the all-purpose flour, coconut flour, baking powder, baking soda, flaxseed meal, vanilla whey protein powder, arrowroot powder, ground ginger, ground cinnamon and sugar.

Mix well.

In another bowl, beat the egg whites. Then, stir in the almond milk, oil, pumpkin puree and vanilla extract.

Add the egg white mixture to the flour mixture.

Stir until moistened.

Let sit for 10 minutes.

Pour the batter into the waffle maker.

Cook according to manufacturer's instructions.

Drizzle the maple syrup over the waffles.

Top with the whipped cream and ground cinnamon.

Nutrients per Serving:

- Calories 196
- Fat 5.8 g
- Saturated fat 0.9 g
- Carbohydrates 25.8 g
- Fiber 5.8 g
- Protein 12.7 g
- Cholesterol 23.3 mg
- Sugars 13 g
- Sodium 338.3 mg
- Potassium 163.4 mg

Strawberry Waffle Sandwich

This waffle sandwich looks like it's going to keep you full throughout the day. And it's true! Not only that, but it's also packed with the nutrients and fiber that you need to keep yourself in shape.

Serving Size: 1

Preparation & Cooking Time: 10 minutes

Ingredients:

- 2 frozen whole wheat waffles
- ½ teaspoon vanilla extract
- ¼ cup ricotta cheese
- 1 teaspoon fresh basil leaves, chopped
- ½ cup fresh strawberries, sliced
- 2 teaspoons maple syrup

Instructions:

Reheat the frozen waffles in your waffle maker.

While waiting, mix the vanilla, ricotta and basil in a bowl.

Spread the ricotta mixture on one side of the waffle.

Top with the strawberries and drizzle with the maple syrup.

Top with the other waffle.

Nutrients per Serving:

- Calories 318
- Fat 8.5 g
- Saturated fat 5.7 g
- Carbohydrates 43.1 g
- Fiber 8.5 g
- Protein 11.9 g
- Cholesterol 31.6 mg
- Sugars 12 g
- Sodium 400.1 mg
- Potassium 359.6 mg

Waffles with Crispy Chicken & Gravy

Impress your family with these simple yet delicious and satisfying savory waffles served with crispy chicken tenders and drenched with creamy gravy.

Serving Size: 4

Preparation & Cooking Time: 1 hour

Ingredients:

Chicken

- Cooking spray
- 2 egg whites
- 1 tablespoon water
- ¾ cup cornflakes, crushed
- ¼ teaspoon dried parsley
- ¼ teaspoon garlic powder
- 2 tablespoons Parmesan cheese, grated
- Pepper to taste
- 12 oz. chicken tenders, sliced into 8

Waffles

- ½ cup whole wheat flour
- ½ cup all-purpose flour
- 1 tablespoon sugar
- ½ teaspoon dried thyme, crushed
- ¾ teaspoon baking powder
- Salt to taste
- 1 egg
- ¾ cup milk
- 2 tablespoons water
- ¼ cup walnuts, toasted and chopped

Gravy

- 2 tablespoons butter
- 2 garlic cloves, minced
- 2 tablespoons all-purpose flour
- ½ cup milk
- ¾ cup chicken broth
- 1 teaspoon fresh thyme, snipped
- 1 teaspoon fresh sage, snipped
- Pepper to taste

Instructions:

Preheat your oven to 425 degrees F.

Spray your baking pan with oil.

In a bowl, beat the egg whites and add water.

In another bowl, combine the cornflakes, dried parsley, garlic powder, Parmesan cheese and pepper.

Dip the chicken strips in the egg whites.

Dredge with the cornflake mixture.

Spray the breaded chicken tenders with oil.

Place the chicken in the baking pan.

Bake in the oven for 20 minutes.

Next, prepare the waffles.

Combine the whole wheat flour, all-purpose flour, sugar, dried thyme, baking powder and salt.

In another bowl, beat the egg, milk and water.

Add this to the flour mixture.

Fold in the walnuts.

Pour the batter into the waffle maker.

Cook according to manufacturer's instructions.

Lastly, prepare the gravy.

In a pan over medium heat, add the butter and cook the garlic for 30 seconds.

Stir in the flour.

Pour in the milk and broth.

Season with the herbs and pepper.

Cook while stirring for 1 minute.

Serve the waffles with the crispy chicken strips and gravy.

Garnish with herb sprigs if you like.

Nutrients per Serving:

- Calories 354
- Fat 12 g
- Saturated fat 4.7 g
- Carbohydrates 33 g
- Fiber 2 g
- Protein 28.8 g
- Cholesterol 72.4 mg
- Sugars 7 g
- Sodium 570.7 mg
- Potassium 591.1 mg

Waffle with Almond Butter, Banana & Choco Chips

This is a simple and easy waffle recipe that you can make even during the busiest time of the day. You can use frozen waffles that you can buy in the groceries or make your own ones and freeze them for later use.

Serving Size: 1

Preparation & Cooking Time: 5 minutes

Ingredients:

- 1 frozen whole grain waffle
- 1 tablespoon almond butter
- ¼ banana, sliced
- 1 teaspoon miniature chocolate chips

Instructions:

Toast the frozen waffle in your waffle maker.

Spread one side with the almond butter.

Top with the banana slices and mini chocolate chips.

Nutrients per Serving:

- Calories 222
- Fat 12.6 g
- Saturated fat 1.7 g
- Carbohydrates 25 g
- Fiber 4.1 g
- Protein 5.3 g
- Cholesterol 0 mg
- Sugars 4.3 g
- Sodium 37 mg
- Potassium 238.4 mg

Ham & Cheese Hash Brown Waffles

These ham and cheese hash brown waffles are truly delightful. You can serve them for breakfast or dinner. It doesn't matter. They are bound to satisfy everyone during mealtime.

Serving Size: 4

Preparation & Cooking Time: 40 minutes

Ingredients:

- 3 eggs
- 1 tablespoon fresh chives, chopped
- 3 garlic cloves, minced
- 2 tablespoons olive oil
- Pepper to taste
- 20 oz. hash browns, shredded
- 1 cup cheddar cheese, shredded
- 1 cup ham, diced

Instructions:

Preheat your waffle maker.

In a bowl, beat the eggs and stir in the chives, garlic, oil and pepper.

Add the hash browns, cheese and ham to the bowl and mix well.

Spread the mixture in your waffle maker.

Bake according to manufacturer's instructions.

Nutrients per Serving:

- Calories 392
- Fat 21.7 g
- Saturated fat 8 g
- Carbohydrates 26.4 g
- Fiber 2.1 g
- Protein 22.8 g
- Cholesterol 185.1 mg
- Sugars 5 g
- Sodium 727.3 mg
- Potassium 605.9 mg

Waffle with Tomato, Spinach & Feta Cheese

Undoubtedly, this waffle is as delicious as it is colorful. And it's very easy to prepare as well. Just use frozen waffles. You can either buy frozen waffles or make your own ones and freeze them, so you can simply reheat when ready to eat. If feta cheese is not available, you can use other types of soft cheese.

Serving Size: 1

Preparation & Cooking Time: 10 minutes

Ingredients:

- 1 frozen whole-wheat waffle
- ¼ cup spinach, sautéed
- 1 tablespoon feta cheese, crumbled
- 3 cherry tomatoes, sliced

Instructions:

Toast the frozen waffle in your waffle iron.

Top with the spinach, cheese and tomatoes.

Serve right away.

Nutrients per Serving:

- Calories 158
- Fat 7.6 g
- Saturated fat 2.3 g
- Carbohydrates 18.5 g
- Fiber 3.2 g
- Protein 5.7 g
- Cholesterol 8.3 mg
- Sugars 10 g
- Sodium 384.5 mg
- Potassium 463.9 mg

Whole Grain Waffle with Cherry Sauce

Make these waffles with cornmeal, which adds an interesting texture. Pour thick cherry sauce on top to complete the meal.

Serving Size: 6

Preparation & Cooking Time: 1 hour

Ingredients:

Sauce

- ¼ cup water
- 2 cups cherries, pitted
- 2 teaspoons cornstarch
- ¼ cup honey
- 1 teaspoon vanilla extract
- 1 teaspoon lemon juice

Waffles

- 2 cups whole wheat flour
- 1 ½ teaspoons baking powder
- ½ teaspoon baking soda
- ½ cup cornmeal
- ¼ teaspoon salt
- 2 eggs
- 2 cups buttermilk
- 1 tablespoon olive oil
- ¼ cup brown sugar
- 2 teaspoons vanilla extract

Instructions:

Add the water, cherries, cornstarch, honey, vanilla extract and lemon juice in a pan over medium heat.

Cook while stirring for 1 minute.

Next, increase temperature to medium high and bring to a boil.

Reduce heat and simmer for 3 minutes. Set aside.

Preheat your waffle maker.

In a bowl, mix the whole wheat flour, baking powder, baking soda, cornmeal and salt.

In another bowl, whisk together the eggs, buttermilk, olive oil, brown sugar and vanilla extract.

Next, add this to the flour mixture and stir.

Add the mixture to the waffle maker.

Then, cook according to the manufacturer's instructions.

Pour the cherry sauce on top of the waffles and serve.

Nutrients per Serving:

- Calories 380
- Fat 5.1 g
- Saturated fat 1.4 g
- Carbohydrates 74.1 g
- Fiber 5.8 g
- Protein 11.6 g
- Cholesterol 65.3 mg
- Sugars 15 g
- Sodium 445 mg
- Potassium 781 mg

Pumpkin Cheesecake Waffles

Spruce up your breakfast with these amazing pumpkin cheesecake waffles that will not disappoint you.

Serving Size: 1

Preparation & Cooking Time: 10 minutes

Ingredients:

- 1 frozen whole grain waffle
- ½ oz. cream cheese
- 1 tablespoon pumpkin puree
- 1 teaspoon walnuts, toasted and chopped

Instructions:

Toast the frozen waffle in your waffle maker.

Spread the cream cheese and pumpkin puree on top.

Sprinkle with the walnuts and serve.

Nutrients per Serving:

- Calories 132
- Fat 7 g
- Saturated fat 2 g
- Carbohydrates 15 g
- Fiber 4 g
- Protein 4 g
- Cholesterol 10 mg
- Sugars 2 g
- Sodium 203 mg
- Potassium 555 mg

Waffle with Egg & Turkey Bacon

With this quick and easy breakfast waffle, you don't have any excuse to skip breakfast. It only takes 10 minutes or less to prepare.

Serving Size: 1

Preparation & Cooking Time: 10 minutes

Ingredients:

- 1 frozen whole grain waffle
- 1 tablespoon olive oil
- 1 egg
- 2 turkey bacon slices
- 1 teaspoon fresh chives, chopped

Instructions:

Toast the frozen waffle in your waffle maker.

Next, add the oil to a pan over medium heat.

Crack the egg and cook until white is set.

Transfer to a plate.

Next, add the turkey bacon and cook until crispy.

Then, top with the waffle with the turkey bacon and egg.

Sprinkle with the chopped chives and serve.

Nutrients per Serving:

- Calories 277
- Fat 17.5 g
- Saturated fat 4.7 g
- Carbohydrates 15.6 g
- Fiber 2.5 g
- Protein 14.2 g
- Cholesterol 202.1 mg
- Sugars 2.7 g
- Sodium 370 mg
- Potassium 163.3 mg

Waffle with Cream Cheese, Granola & Plums

Start your day on a tasty note with this waffle topped with cream cheese, granola and plums.

Serving Size: 1

Preparation & Cooking Time: 5 minutes

Ingredients:

- 1 frozen whole grain waffle
- 1 tablespoon cream cheese
- 1 tablespoon granola
- 1 plum, sliced

Instructions:

Toast the frozen waffle in your waffle iron.

Spread the cream cheese on top.

Sprinkle the granola and arrange the plums on top.

Serve immediately.

Nutrients per Serving:

- Calories 188
- Fat 9.6 g
- Saturated fat 3.5 g
- Carbohydrates 24.9 g
- Fiber 4.8 g
- Protein 4.4 g
- Cholesterol 14.6 mg
- Sugars 5 g
- Sodium 218.9 mg
- Potassium 225.4 mg

Oat & Poppy Seed Waffles with Citrus

These fiber-packed waffles are not only nutritious but also crunchy and tasty. Everyone will love having them in the morning.

Serving Size: 8

Preparation & Cooking Time: 45 minutes

Ingredients:

Syrup

- 2 oranges
- ½ cup water
- 1 tablespoon honey
- 1 tablespoon lemon juice
- 1 tablespoon cornstarch

Waffle

- ½ cup oat bran
- ⅓ cup whole wheat flour
- ⅔ cup all-purpose flour
- 2 tablespoons flaxseed meal
- 1 ½ teaspoons baking powder
- 2 teaspoons poppy seeds
- 1 tablespoon sugar
- Salt to taste
- 1 egg
- 3 tablespoons canola oil
- ¾ cup milk
- 1 teaspoon vanilla extract
- ¼ cup water

Instructions:

Peel the oranges and slice into segments.

Squeeze half of the orange segments to extract the juice.

Add the orange juice to a pan over medium heat.

Stir in the water, honey, lemon juice and cornstarch.

Simmer for 3 to 4 minutes.

Prepare the waffles by mixing the oat bran, all-purpose flour, whole wheat flour, flaxseed meal, baking powder, poppy seeds, sugar and salt in a bowl.

In another bowl, whisk together the egg, canola oil, milk, vanilla extract and water.

Add this mixture to the oat bran mixture.

Pour the batter into your waffle maker.

Cook according to manufacturer's instructions.

Serve with the reserved orange slices.

Nutrients per Serving:

- Calories 173
- Fat 6.7 g
- Saturated fat 0.5 g
- Carbohydrates 26.3 g
- Fiber 3.2 g
- Protein 5.1 g
- Cholesterol 0.5 mg
- Sugars 8.3 g
- Sodium 189.6 mg
- Potassium 179.1 mg

Waffle Topped with Blueberry & Crispy Bacon Bits

This waffle is proof that healthy and delicious can go together. Blueberry supplies you with the nutrients that you need, while bacon obviously makes the waffle even more delicious.

Serving Size: 1

Preparation & Cooking Time: 10 minutes

Ingredients:

- 1 frozen waffle
- 2 bacon slices, cooked crisp and crumbled
- ¼ cup fresh blueberries
- 4 teaspoons pecans, toasted and chopped
- 2 teaspoons maple syrup

Instructions:

Toast the frozen waffle in your waffle iron.

Top with the crumbled bacon, blueberries and pecans.

Drizzle with the maple syrup and serve.

Nutrients per Serving:

- Calories 211
- Fat 12 g
- Saturated fat 2 g
- Carbohydrates 21 g
- Fiber 5 g
- Protein 8 g
- Cholesterol 7 mg
- Sugars 10 g
- Sodium 312 mg
- Potassium 778 mg

Carrot Cake Waffle Sandwich

Yes, you can have a carrot cake for breakfast when you make this fantastic carrot cake waffle sandwich. It will only take you 5 minutes to prepare if you use frozen waffles.

Serving Size: 1

Preparation & Cooking Time: 5 minutes

Ingredients:

- 2 frozen whole grain waffles
- 2 tablespoons cream cheese
- ½ cup carrot, shredded
- 1 tablespoon walnuts, toasted and chopped
- 2 tablespoons raisins
- 2 teaspoons maple syrup

Instructions:

Toast the frozen waffles in your waffle maker.

Spread one side of the waffle with the cream cheese.

Top with the carrot, walnuts, and raisins.

Drizzle with the maple syrup.

Top with the other waffle and serve.

Nutrients per Serving:

- Calories 441
- Fat 20.1 g
- Saturated fat 6.4 g
- Carbohydrates 56.5 g
- Fiber 4.7 g
- Protein 12.8 g
- Cholesterol 95.4 mg
- Sugars 10 g
- Sodium 400 mg
- Potassium 604.5 mg

Chocolate & Coffee Waffles with Raisins

These rich and decadent chocolate and coffee waffles will make your tummy happy and your heart sing!

Serving Size: 8

Preparation & Cooking Time: 30 minutes

Ingredients:

- 1 ½ cups all-purpose flour
- ½ teaspoon salt
- ½ teaspoon baking soda
- 1 ½ teaspoons baking powder
- ⅔ cup cocoa powder
- 2 cups buttermilk
- 1 egg, beaten
- 1 tablespoon canola oil
- ¾ cup brown sugar
- 2 teaspoons vanilla extract
- 1 teaspoon instant coffee granules

For serving

- Chocolate syrup
- Raisins

Instructions:

Preheat your waffle maker.

In a bowl, combine the all-purpose flour, baking powder, baking soda, cocoa powder and salt.

In another bowl, mix the buttermilk, egg, oil, brown sugar and vanilla extract.

Add this to the flour mixture.

Stir in the coffee granules.

Pour the batter into the waffle maker.

Cook according to manufacturer's instructions.

Drizzle with the chocolate syrup and top with the raisins before serving.

Nutrients per Serving:

- Calories 226
- Fat 4.1 g
- Saturated fat 1.3 g
- Carbohydrates 43.7 g
- Fiber 3.2 g
- Protein 6.9 g
- Cholesterol 25.5 mg
- Sugars 17 g
- Sodium 436.1 mg
- Potassium 265 mg

Cornbread Waffles

These cornbread waffles are so easy to make that even when you're running late in the morning, you can still find time to eat the healthy breakfast.

Serving Size: 6

Preparation & Cooking Time: 35 minutes

Ingredients:

- 1 cup all-purpose flour
- 1 ½ teaspoons baking powder
- 1 teaspoon baking soda
- 1 ½ cups yellow cornmeal
- Salt to taste
- 2 eggs
- ½ cup butter, melted
- 1 cup buttermilk
- 1 teaspoon honey
- 6 tablespoons sugar

For serving

- Softened butter
- Honey

Instructions:

Preheat your waffle maker.

In a bowl, combine the all-purpose flour, baking powder, baking soda, cornmeal and salt.

Beat the eggs in another bowl.

Stir in the butter, milk, honey and sugar.

Add this to the flour mixture.

Mix until moistened.

Add the batter to the waffle maker.

Cook according to manufacturer's instructions.

Top with the butter and drizzle with the honey before serving.

Nutrients per Serving:

- Calories 410
- Fat 18.6 g
- Saturated Fat 10.6 g
- Carbohydrate 55 g
- Fiber 2.8 g
- Protein 8 g
- Cholesterol 97 mg
- Sugars 15.3 g
- Sodium 422 mg
- Potassium 323 mg

Red Velvet Waffles

These red velvet waffles will make everyone at the breakfast table go wow. They are as tasty as they are vibrant.

Serving Size: 6

Preparation & Cooking Time: 30 minutes

Ingredients:

- 1 pack red velvet cake mix
- 2 cups milk
- 4 eggs, beaten
- 4 tablespoons cream cheese, softened
- 2 cups powdered sugar
- Whipped cream
- ½ cup miniature chocolate chips

Instructions:

First, preheat your waffle maker.

Combine the cake mix, milk and eggs.

Mix until smooth.

Next, in another bowl, mix the cream cheese and sugar.

Add this to the cake mix.

Add the batter to the waffle iron.

Cook according to manufacturer's instructions.

Lastly, top with the whipped cream and chocolate chips.

Nutrients per Serving:

- Calories 623
- Fat 16 g
- Saturated Fat 6.4 g
- Carbohydrate 110.6 g
- Fiber 0 g
- Protein 10.8 g
- Cholesterol 123 mg
- Sugars 81.2 g
- Sodium 622 mg
- Potassium 95 mg

Mac & Cheese Waffles

Turn your favorite mac and cheese into crispy waffle bites using this simple-to-follow recipe that takes less than an hour to prepare.

Serving Size: 10

Preparation & Cooking Time: 40 minutes

Ingredients:

- 6 oz. box macaroni and cheese, prepared according to package instructions
- ¼ cup milk
- 1/3 cup breadcrumbs
- 1 egg, beaten
- 1 ½ cups cheddar cheese, shredded

Instructions:

Combine all the ingredients in a bowl.

Add the mixture to your waffle maker.

Cook according to manufacturer's instructions.

Slice into smaller pieces before serving.

Nutrients per Serving:

- Calories 216
- Fat 10.1 g
- Saturated Fat 5.2 g
- Carbohydrate 20.6 g
- Fiber 0.9 g
- Protein 10.6 g
- Cholesterol 44 mg
- Sugars 1.4 g
- Sodium 777 mg
- Potassium 160 mg

Omelet Waffles

Yes, you can cook an omelet in your waffle maker! Add ham, cheese and chopped chives to your eggs to make your omelet savory and tasty.

Serving Size: 1

Preparation & Cooking Time: 10 minutes

Ingredients:

- 3 eggs
- ¼ cup cheddar cheese, shredded
- 2 tablespoons ham, cooked and chopped
- 2 teaspoons parsley, chopped
- Salt and pepper to taste

Instructions:

Beat the eggs in a bowl.

Stir in the cheese and ham.

Season with the parsley, salt and pepper.

Add the mixture to your waffle maker.

Cook according to manufacturer's instructions.

Serve immediately.

Nutrients per Serving:

- Calories 331
- Fat 24 g
- Saturated Fat 10.6 g
- Carbohydrate 2.3 g
- Fiber 0.3 g
- Protein 26.5 g
- Cholesterol 530 mg
- Sugars 1.2 g
- Sodium 582 mg
- Potassium 268 mg

Mozzarella Waffles

Mozzarella sticks are a popular appetizer all over the world. You can make them in your waffle maker using this recipe.

Serving Size: 8

Preparation & Cooking Time: 30 minutes

Ingredients:

- 1 cup all-purpose flour
- 2 eggs, beaten
- 2 tablespoons milk
- 1 cup Italian bread crumbs
- Salt to taste
- 16 mozzarella sticks

For garnish

- Chopped parsley
- Shredded Parmesan cheese

For serving

- Marinara sauce

Instructions:

Preheat your waffle maker.

Add the all-purpose flour to a bowl.

Next, in a second bowl, beat the eggs and milk.

In a third bowl, mix the breadcrumbs and salt.

Cover the mozzarella sticks with the flour.

Next, dip in the egg mixture.

Dredge with the breadcrumbs.

Add these to the waffle maker.

Then, cook for 4 to 5 minutes or until golden and crispy.

Garnish with the chopped parsley and Parmesan cheese.

Serve with the marinara sauce.

Nutrients per Serving:

Calories 290

- Fat 12.1 g
- Saturated Fat 6.7 g
- Carbohydrate 24.2 g
- Dietary Fiber 0.9 g
- Protein 21.1 g
- Cholesterol 71 mg
- Sugars 1.3 g
- Sodium 602 mg
- Potassium 34 mg

Cauliflower Waffles

These cauliflower waffles are surprisingly good. They are a good way to sneak in vegetables to kids' breakfast.

Serving Size: 1

Preparation & Cooking Time: 20 minutes

Ingredients:

- 3 cups cauliflower, grated
- 3 cups mozzarella cheese, shredded
- ½ cup Parmesan cheese, shredded
- 3 eggs
- ¼ cup cornstarch
- 1 teaspoon paprika
- Salt and pepper to taste

Instructions:

Combine all the ingredients in a bowl.

Pour the batter into your waffle maker.

Cook according to manufacturer's instructions.

Serve with egg or bacon.

Nutrients per Serving:

- Calories 339
- Fat 15.9 g
- Saturated Fat 7.6 g
- Carbohydrate 25.4 g
- Fiber 4.3 g
- Protein 25.7 g
- Cholesterol 273 mg
- Sugars 4.2 g
- Sodium 459 mg
- Potassium 569 mg

French Toast Waffles

These dreamy waffles are actually easier to make than you imagine. Just follow the recipe and you can enjoy the heavenly dessert within only a few minutes.

Serving Size: 4

Preparation & Cooking Time: 25 minutes

Ingredients:

- 2 tablespoons strawberry jam
- ¼ cup strawberries, chopped
- 8 tablespoons cream cheese
- 2 eggs, beaten
- ½ cup milk
- 1 tablespoon sugar
- ¼ teaspoon ground nutmeg
- ½ teaspoon cinnamon powder
- 8 frozen waffles

For serving

- Maple syrup
- Confectioners' sugar

Instructions:

Mix the strawberries, strawberry jam and cream cheese in a bowl.

In another bowl, combine the eggs, milk, sugar, ground nutmeg and cinnamon powder.

Dip the frozen waffles in this mixture and add to the waffle maker.

Toast the waffles according to manufacturer's instructions.

Spread the waffles with the strawberry mixture and stack together.

Drizzle with the maple syrup and dust with confectioners' sugar.

Nutrients per Serving:

- Calories 677
- Fat 39.5 g
- Saturated Fat 21.9 g
- Sodium 418 mg
- Carbohydrate 61.1 g
- Fiber 0.8g
- Protein 21.4 g
- Cholesterol 425 mg
- Sugars 20.3 g
- Potassium 340 mg

Oreo Cake Waffles

You'll love this waffle cake that's made with Oreos, cream cheese filling and chocolate. Every slice of it is a big treat for your sweet tooth.

Serving Size: 2

Preparation & Cooking Time: 30 minutes

Ingredients:

- 2 frozen chocolate waffles
- 1 cup heavy cream
- 8 oz. cream cheese, softened
- 8 Oreo cookies, crushed
- ½ cup powdered sugar

For topping

- Oreo cookies
- Whipped cream

Instructions:

Toast the frozen waffles in the waffle iron.

In a bowl, mix the heavy cream, cream cheese, crushed Oreos and powdered sugar.

Spread the cream mixture on top of one waffle.

Top with the other waffle.

Spread the whipped cream topping on top and sprinkle with the remaining Oreos.

Nutrients per Serving:

- Calories 504
- Fat 36.3 g
- Saturated Fat 20.4 g
- Carbohydrate 39.8 g
- Fiber 1 g
- Protein 7.2 g
- Cholesterol 106 mg
- Sugars 23.8 g
- Sodium 396 mg
- Potassium 151 mg

Beignet Waffles

Beignets are French donuts that are truly delightful to have at any time during the day. You can make the waffle version of them using this recipe.

Serving Size: 16

Preparation & Cooking Time: 1 hour

Ingredients:

Donuts

- ½ teaspoon baking soda
- 2 teaspoons baking powder
- 2 cups all-purpose flour
- ¾ cup granulated sugar
- 1 teaspoon salt
- 2 teaspoons ground cinnamon
- 2 eggs
- ¼ cup butter, melted
- ¾ cup buttermilk
- 1 teaspoon vanilla extract
- 2 cups apples, chopped
- Oil for frying

Glaze

- 1 ½ cups powdered sugar
- ¼ cup milk
- 2 teaspoons vanilla extract

Instructions:

First, mix the flour, baking soda, baking powder, sugar, salt and ground cinnamon in a bowl.

Second, in another bowl, beat the eggs, butter, milk and vanilla extract.

Next, add the egg mixture to the flour mixture and mix well.

Fold in the apples.

Pour the mixture into the waffle maker.

Bake according to the manufacturer's instructions.

Let cool and slice into smaller portions.

Next, add the oil to a pan over medium high heat.

Fry the waffles for 1 to 2 minutes per side.

Then, drain on a plate lined with paper towel.

Mix the glaze ingredients.

Dip the waffles in the glaze.

Let cool for 20 minutes before serving.

Nutrients per Serving:

- Calories 191
- Fat 4 g
- Saturated fat 2 g
- Carbohydrates 36 g
- Fiber 1 g
- Protein 3 g
- Cholesterol 30 mg
- Sugars 23 g
- Sodium 203 mg
- Potassium 112 mg

Strawberry Waffles with Maple Whipped Cream

This is the waffle version of the famous strawberry shortcake. You're going to enjoy serving it to your friends who will only have wonderful things to say about the sweet treat.

Serving Size: 4

Preparation & Cooking Time: 30 minutes

Ingredients:

Waffle

- 2 cups buttermilk pancake mix
- 1 cup fresh strawberries, chopped
- 2 eggs, beaten
- 1 ½ cups milk
- ¼ cup olive oil

Maple whipped cream

- 1 cup heavy whipping cream
- 2 tablespoons pure maple syrup

For serving

- Fresh strawberries, sliced

Instructions:

Preheat your waffle maker.

In a bowl, combine the buttermilk pancake mix, chopped strawberries, eggs, milk and olive oil.

Mix well.

Pour the batter into your waffle maker.

Cook according to the manufacturer's instructions.

Beat the heavy whipping cream using an electric mixer on high speed until thickened.

Stir in the maple syrup and mix until fluffy.

Layer the waffles with the maple cream and fresh strawberry slices.

Nutrients per Serving:

- Calories 466
- Fat 29.9 g
- Saturated Fat 10.8 g
- Carbohydrate 41 g
- Fiber 2.2 g
- Protein 10.6 g
- Cholesterol 135 mg
- Sugars 17.5 g
- Sodium 442 mg
- Potassium 180 mg

Gingerbread Yogurt Waffles

Stack your gingerbread waffles and layer them with cream sauce for breakfast or dessert that will surely brighten up your day.

Serving Size: 4

Preparation & Cooking Time: 15 minutes

Ingredients:

- ¾ cup whole wheat flour
- 1 cup all-purpose flour
- 1 tablespoon baking powder
- 1 teaspoon ground ginger
- 1 teaspoon ground cinnamon
- ¼ cup brown sugar
- ½ teaspoon salt
- 3 eggs, beaten
- 1 cup milk
- ½ cup butter, melted
- ½ cup plain yogurt
- ¼ cup molasses

Glaze

- ¼ cup milk
- ¼ cup cream
- 2 cups powdered sugar
- ½ teaspoon vanilla extract

Instructions:

Preheat your waffle maker.

Add the all-purpose flour, whole wheat flour, baking powder, ground ginger, ground cinnamon, brown sugar and salt to a bowl.

Stir to combine.

In another bowl, whisk together the eggs, milk, butter, yogurt and molasses.

Add this to the flour mixture.

Transfer the batter to your waffle maker.

Cook according to manufacturer's instructions.

Prepare the glaze by mixing the milk, cream, powdered sugar and vanilla extract.

Stack the waffles and layer with the cream sauce.

Nutrients per Serving:

- Calories 565
- Fat 19.6 g
- Saturated Fat 11.5 g
- Carbohydrate 89.5 g
- Fiber 1.3 g
- Protein 9.3 g
- Cholesterol 129 mg
- Sugars 56.4 g
- Sodium 381 mg
- Potassium 616 mg

Conclusion

It is easy to appreciate the simplicity and versatility of waffles through their history.

After all, we can agree that waffles are delicious. However, the way we want them done, we can't deny just how much sweeter life is with waffles for breakfast or at any time of the day.

It's a good thing that you now have this cookbook whenever you have an instant waffle craving.

Have fun!

Author's Afterthoughts

I want to convey my big thanks to all of my readers who have taken the time to read my book. Readers like you make my work so rewarding and I cherish each and every one of you.

Grateful cannot describe how I feel when I know that someone has chosen my work over all of the choices available online. I hope you enjoyed the book as much as I enjoyed writing it.

Feedback from my readers is how I grow and learn as a chef and an author. Please take the time to let me know your thoughts by leaving a review on Amazon so I and your fellow readers can learn from your experience.

My deepest thanks,

Sophia Freeman

https://sophia.subscribemenow.com/

Printed in Great Britain
by Amazon

66252978R00097